Cheryl Ford

THE STORY OF THE DALLAS WINGS

Marina Mabrey

WNBA: A HISTORY OF WOMEN'S HOOPS

THE STORY OF THE

DALLAS WINGS

JIM WHITING

Alexis Hornbuckle

CREATIVE EDUCATION / CREATIVE PAPERBACKS

Published by Creative Education and Creative Paperbacks
P.O. Box 227, Mankato, Minnesota 56002
Creative Education and Creative Paperbacks are imprints of
The Creative Company
www.thecreativecompany.us

Design and production by Blue Design (www.bluedes.com)
Art direction by Rita Marshall

Photographs by AP Images (Ross D. Franklin, Jason Redmond, Paul Warner),
Getty (Leon Bennett, Domenic Centofanti, Tim Clayton/Corbis, Icon
Sportswire, Meg Oliphant, Christian Petersen, Tom Pidgeon, The Washington
Post)

Library of Congress Cataloging-in-Publication Data
Names: Whiting, Jim, 1943- author.
Title: The story of the Dallas Wings / by Jim Whiting.
Description: Mankato, Minnesota : Creative Education and Creative
    Paperbacks, [2024] | Series: Creative sports. WNBA : A History of
    Women's Hoops. | Includes index. | Audience: Ages 8-12 | Audience:
    Grades 4-6 | Summary: "Middle grade basketball fans are introduced to
    the extraordinary history of WNBA's Dallas Wings with a photo-laden
    narrative of their greatest successes and losses"-- Provided by
    publisher.
Identifiers: LCCN 2022034240 (print) | LCCN 2022034241 (ebook) | ISBN
    9781640267190 (library binding) | ISBN 9781682772751 (paperback) | ISBN
    9781640008700 (pdf)
Subjects: LCSH: Dallas Wings (Basketball team)--History--Juvenile
    literature. | CYAC: Basketball players. | Basketball teams.
Classification: LCC GV885.52.D35 W55 2024 (print) | LCC GV885.52.D35
    (ebook) | DDC 796.323/64097642812--dc23/eng/20220826
LC record available at https://lccn.loc.gov/2022034240
LC ebook record available at https://lccn.loc.gov/2022034241

Printed in China

Skylar Diggins-Smith

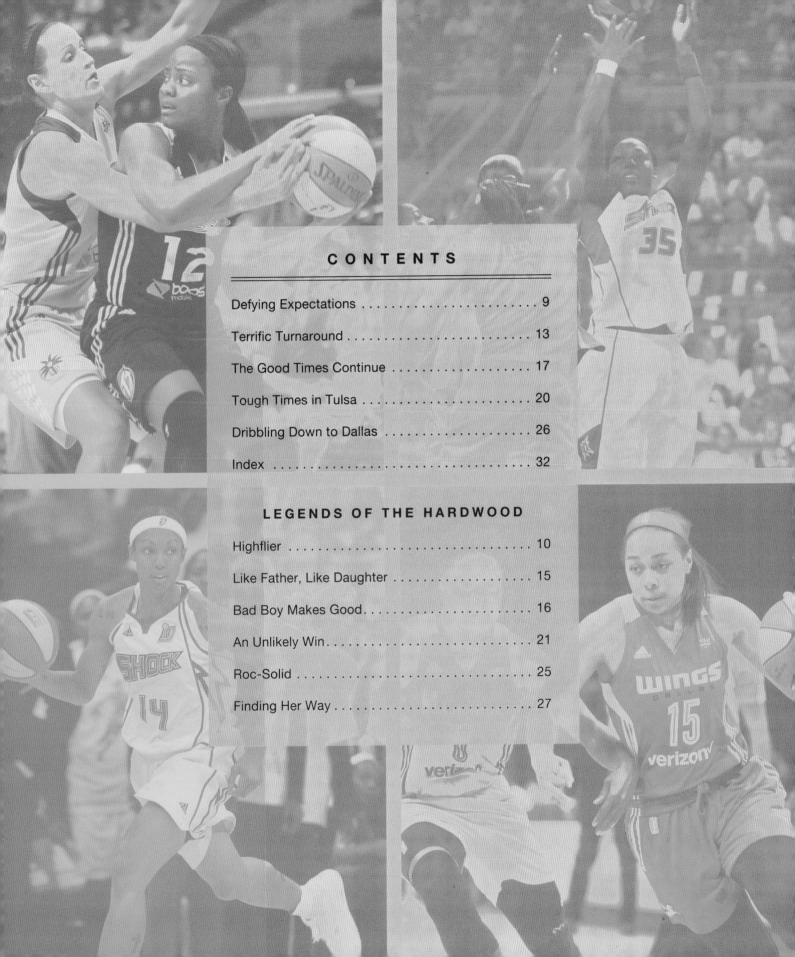

CONTENTS

LEGENDS OF THE HARDWOOD

The Dallas Wings hosted the New York Liberty on September 11, 2021. A Dallas win would clinch a playoff berth in the Women's National Basketball Association (WNBA) playoffs for the first time in three years. The Liberty led 70–57 early in the fourth quarter. Dallas battled back. Forward Kayla Thornton grabbed an offensive rebound and put the ball into the basket. That knotted the score at 70–70. Minutes later, New York broke the tie with a basket. They led 72–70. Dallas guard Marina Mabrey hit two free throws. That tied the score again. New York regained the lead on two free throws. With two minutes left, Dallas forward Satou Sabally hit a three-point shot. It put Dallas ahead 75–74. Her lay-in soon afterward gave the Wings a three-point lead. New York narrowed the margin to one point with 29 seconds left. Dallas missed a three-point attempt with eight seconds left. New York grabbed the rebound. With one second remaining, Wings guard Allisha Gray blocked a Liberty shot. Dallas won 77–76. They were in the playoffs!

Kayla Thornton

LEGENDS OF THE HARDWOOD

DEANNA NOLAN
GUARD
HEIGHT: 5-FOOT-9
SHOCK SEASONS: 2001–09

HIGHFLIER

Deanna Nolan led her Michigan high school team to state championships in 1994 and 1995. She was named the state's Miss Basketball. Her quickness and 34-inch vertical leap led to her nickname of "Tweety," after the Looney Tunes cartoon character Tweety Bird. "She's so cute and flies like I can," Nolan explained. Nolan helped the University of Georgia to the NCAA Women's Final Four in 1999. The Shock made her the sixth overall draft choice in 2001. She came off the bench in her first season to average more than seven points per game. She started every game for the next eight seasons and averaged more than 13 points a game. Nolan was a five-time All-Star and made the All-WNBA First or Second Team five times. In 2016, she was named one of the WNBA's top 20 players in its 20 seasons.

Deanna Nolan

The Wings date back more than 20 years to a different city and a different name. The WNBA began play in 1997 with eight teams. The league added two more teams the following season. One was in Detroit, Michigan. At that time, WNBA teams were connected to National Basketball Association (NBA) teams. Detroit is associated with the automobile industry. Its NBA team is the Detroit Pistons. The new WNBA team's name also focused on an automobile part: shock absorbers. It became the Detroit Shock.

Most professional sports teams struggle in their first season. The Shock lost their first four games but came on strong the rest of the season. They finished 17–13. Guard Korie Hlede averaged 14 points a game. She was runner-up in voting for WNBA Rookie of the Year. Detroit missed the playoffs by one game. But as coach Nancy Lieberman-Cline said, "We are setting standards that all expansion teams will be measured by."

Detroit hovered around the .500 level in 1999. They finished 15–17. Guard Sandy Brondello averaged more than 13 points a game. She was named to the All-Star Game. Detroit finished in a three-way tie for second in the WNBA's Eastern Conference. The Shock made the playoffs through a tiebreaker. The first round was a single game. Detroit fell 60–54 to the Charlotte Sting.

The Shock finished 14–18 in 2000. They tied the Washington Mystics for the final playoff slot. The tiebreaker favored the Mystics. In 2001, Detroit split their first six games. They followed that with a five-game losing streak. They never recovered and finished 10–22. The team's top draft pick had been guard Deanna Nolan. She would play a key role in reversing those numbers in the coming seasons.

TERRIFIC TURNAROUND

The Shock began 2002 by losing their first 10 games. Bill Laimbeer became coach. He was a former player who helped the Pistons win two NBA titles with his hard-nosed style. He had never coached before. The Shock lost their first game under him by 21 points. Two more losses followed before the first victory. The team finished 9–23.

The 2003 season began with a three-point loss. Then the Shock rattled off eight wins in a row. They had another winning streak of five games and two more streaks of four. They finished 25–9. It is the greatest one-season turnaround in WNBA history. Forward Cheryl Ford averaged nearly 11 points a game. She was named WNBA Rookie of the Year. Nolan averaged more than 12 points a game. Second-year forward Swin Cash averaged nearly 17 points and 6 rebounds a game. She was named to the All-WNBA First Team and All-Star Game.

The Shock defeated the Cleveland Rockers in the conference semifinals. They swept the Connecticut Sun in the conference finals. Now they faced the two-time defending champion Los Angeles Sparks in the best-of-three WNBA Finals. Los Angeles rode a huge first half lead of 42–21 to a 75–63 win in Game 1. Detroit had a 19-point second-half lead in Game 2. They couldn't hold it. The Sparks led 61–57 with 1:28 left. Shock guard Kedra Holland-Corn sank a three-pointer. It brought Detroit to within a point. Nolan hit two free throws with 12 seconds remaining. The Shock hung on. They won 62–61.

Cheryl Ford

Game 3 in Detroit had 22,076 fans. It is the largest crowd in WNBA history. The game featured two All-Star centers. Detroit's Ruth Riley outscored Lisa Leslie of the Sparks, 27–13. The Shock won 83–78. They were WNBA champions! No team in U.S. pro sports had ever gone from the worst record in its league one year to the championship the next. Riley gave credit to Laimbeer. "He gave us the wisdom that he had as a player, that we just have a lot of heart, we love to play together," she said.

The Shock finished 17–17 in 2004. They faced the New York Liberty in the conference semifinals. The teams split the first two games. Detroit built a 15-point second-half lead in Game 3. New York came back to tie. A Liberty shot with 0.5 seconds remaining gave them a 66–64 series-clinching win. The Shock began 2005 with a 5–1 mark. But they ended 16–18. Connecticut swept them in the conference semifinals.

Detroit Shock 2003 WNBA championship celebration

CHERYL FORD
FORWARD
HEIGHT: 6-FOOT-3
SHOCK SEASONS: 2003–09

LIKE FATHER, LIKE DAUGHTER

Cheryl Ford was probably destined to be a basketball star. Her
father is Karl Malone. He is the third all-time leading scorer
in NBA history. Her talent wasn't immediately obvious. "I
was a tall and skinny and lanky girl that had no coordination
or nothing," she said. Her mother urged her to join a local
basketball team. The coach saw Ford's potential. He helped her
make rapid progress. Ford followed in her father's footsteps to
Louisiana Tech University. She was an All-American Honorable
Mention. Detroit made her the third overall pick in the 2003
WNBA Draft. She became one of a handful of rookies to average
more than 10 points and 10 rebounds per game in a season. She
was named WNBA Rookie of the Year. Ford started every game
in her Detroit career. She played in four All-Star Games.

DALLAS WINGS

Bill Laimbeer

LEGENDS
OF THE HARDWOOD

BILL LAIMBEER
HEAD COACH
SHOCK SEASONS:
2002–09

BAD BOY MAKES GOOD

The Detroit Pistons of the late 1980s and early 1990s were nicknamed "Bad Boys" for their extremely physical play. Center Bill Laimbeer was the "baddest" of them. Many rivals thought he was too aggressive. Laimbeer explained, "I'm playing to win, and I'll use all my tools both physically and mentally to win the game. Other players don't like that." Few players were more disliked around the league. When Laimbeer retired, Horace Grant—a longtime opponent—said, "There's going to be a big party at my house tonight. Everybody's invited." Grant didn't mean it as a compliment. Yet Laimbeer was a four-time All-Star. He averaged more than 13 points and 10 rebounds per game. The Shock hired him as a special consultant before the 2002 season. Soon afterward, he became coach. He led the team to three WNBA titles.

THE GOOD TIMES CONTINUE

Detroit rebounded in 2006 with a 23–11 record. They easily defeated the Indiana Fever in the conference semifinals. They faced the Connecticut Sun in the conference finals. Connecticut had lost just eight games during the regular season. Three came from the Shock. Detroit continued its dominance. They won the series, 2 games to 1.

Detroit took on the defending champion Sacramento Monarchs in the WNBA Finals. It was the first time the series had been best-of-five games. The Monarchs blew out Detroit in Game 1. The Shock came back to win Game 2, 73–63. Sacramento had another blowout win in Game 3. Detroit thrashed the Monarchs in Game 4, 72–52. In Game 5, Sacramento had a 44–36 halftime lead. The Shock outscored Sacramento, 22–9, in the third quarter. They held a narrow 78–75 lead in the game's final seconds. Detroit star guard Katie Smith hit a jump shot. It gave the Shock an 80–75 win and the WNBA title. "Katie's a great, great player and she did just what we expected her to do," said Laimbeer.

Detroit roared out to a 10–1 start in 2007. They finished 24–10. New York crushed the Shock, 73–51, in Game 1 of the conference semifinals. Detroit won Game 2 by three points and Game 3 by one in overtime to take the series. They faced the Fever in the conference finals. Indiana won Game 1. Detroit easily won the next two.

The Shock faced the Phoenix Mercury in the WNBA Finals. Detroit won Game 1. The Mercury trounced them in Game 2. Detroit won Game 3. Phoenix took a back-

and-forth Game 4, 77–76, to even the series. The game had 7 ties and 14 lead changes. The Mercury took a 55–43 halftime edge in Game 5. They won 108–92 to claim the championship.

Detroit started 2008 with a six-game winning streak. They cruised to a 22–12 overall mark. They edged the Fever in the conference semifinals, 2 games to 1. New York won the first game in the conference finals. Detroit came back to win the next two.

The Shock took on the San Antonio Silver Stars in the WNBA Finals. They opened with a 77–69 win and took Game 2, 69–61. Game 3 was tight for the first three quarters. Detroit outscored San Antonio, 27–15, in the final quarter. They won, 76–60. Detroit became the second WNBA team to win three titles. The Houston Comets had won the first four championships.

Laimbeer resigned three games into the 2009 season. He wanted to pursue NBA coaching opportunities. The Shock went 18–16. They opened the playoffs by sweeping the Atlanta Dream in the conference semifinals. They easily won Game 1 over the Fever in the conference finals. Indiana had narrow wins in the next two games.

Alexis Hornbuckle

TOUGH TIMES IN TULSA

The Shock had a problem in Detroit. There were four other professional teams there. The team had trouble getting fans to come to their games. The Shock's owners decided to move to Tulsa, Oklahoma. The closest pro team was the Oklahoma City Thunder. It was nearly 100 miles away. Owners kept the Shock name. "I think it's clear the Shock name resonated with fans because of the championship history it involves, as well as the feelings of speed and power it brings," said team official Steve Swetoha.

The team didn't keep their winning edge. Several key players, such as Ford, Nolan, and Smith, refused to make the move. "I've played with the Shock my entire career and thought it would end there," Nolan explained. "I didn't want to play nowhere else." If the team's change in wins between 2002 and 2003 was the best turnaround in league history, 2009 to 2010 was one of the worst. Tulsa started 3–3. Then they lost 12 in a row. After a win, they lost the next seven. They finished 6–28.

The Shock did even worse in 2011. WNBA legend Sheryl Swoopes came out of retirement to play her final season in Tulsa. She had been the first WNBA player with 6,000 points. But she was 40 years old and couldn't carry the team. Tulsa lost their first five games. After a win, they dropped the next 20 over a span of more than 2 months. It is the longest losing streak in league history. After two wins, they ended the season with six more losses. The final 3–31 record is the worst

LEGENDS
OF THE HARDWOOD

AN UNLIKELY WIN

The Shock had lost a WNBA-record 20 games in a row. This game in Los Angeles seemed likely to extend the streak. Tulsa had lost to the Sparks at home five days earlier. They had also lost 13 straight road games. "I'm sure no one gave us a shot to win this game," said veteran Tulsa forward Sheryl Swoopes. The Shock trailed the Sparks just 60-56 after three quarters. Tulsa took a six-point lead midway in the fourth quarter. The Sparks tied the score at 75–75 with 26 seconds remaining. After a timeout, Swoopes wound down the clock. With 2.9 seconds left, she drained a jump shot. It gave Tulsa a 77–75 lead. The Sparks missed a desperation heave. The losing streak was finally over! "It's unbelievable," coach Teresa Edwards said. "I was waiting to see if we were ever going to get one."

DALLAS WINGS

in league history in terms of winning percentage (.088). It is also the most losses.

The 2012 season began the same way the previous one had ended. The Shock lost their first nine games. It took seven more games just to match the previous season's win total of three. They finished 9–25.

The 2013 season was like the previous three. Once again wins were hard to come by as Tulsa compiled an 11–23 record. One bright spot was guard Riquna Williams. She set a single-game WNBA scoring record with 51 points. Another standout was guard Skylar Diggins. Before the season, the league had promoted her as one of "Three to See." These were three rookies with outstanding college careers. Diggins averaged nearly nine points and four assists. She was named to the WNBA All-Rookie First Team. The 2014 season began with five straight losses. Three times soon afterward, the Shock came within a game of rising to the .500 level. They fell back each time and finished 12–22.

Things finally turned around in 2015. After losing their opener, the Shock ran off eight wins in a row. But soon afterward, a 10-game losing streak dropped their record to 10–14. They rebounded to win six in a row. They finished 18–16. For the first time since moving to Tulsa, the Shock were in the playoffs. They faced the Phoenix Mercury in the Western Conference semifinals. Phoenix crushed them in the best-of-three series, 88–55 and 91–67, respectively.

Jordan Hooper

SKYLAR DIGGINS-SMITH
GUARD
HEIGHT: 5-FOOT-9
SHOCK/WINGS SEASONS: 2013–18

ROC-SOLID

Skylar Diggins-Smith became the first female athlete to join hip-hop artist Jay-Z's Roc National Sports agency. It has helped her gain endorsement deals with companies such as BodyArmor sports drink and shoe giant Puma. These deals provide her with an income several times larger than her WNBA salary. It has another benefit besides the money. WNBA salaries are relatively low. Many players play in overseas leagues to earn extra money. Diggins-Smith doesn't need to. "Being able to be here in the United States year-round is a blessing," she said. "[I] have that duality of being in the WNBA in the spring and summer and then being able to focus a lot of my time as a businesswoman in the off-season."

DALLAS WINGS

DRIBBLING DOWN TO DALLAS

Before the 2015 season ended, team officials decided to move to Dallas, Texas. The fan base was larger, and Dallas had a much larger media market. "I am proud of the team and the organization and know they will stay focused on making this a winning season," said owner Bill Cameron. The team name changed to Wings, after the Greek mythological flying horse Pegasus. In 1934, the Dallas-based Magnolia Petroleum Company had put a Pegasus neon sign on top of its headquarters building. It became the unofficial symbol of Dallas. "It's a durable icon that represents this community," said team official David Swartzell. "It's those powerful wings that ultimately personify what our team is all about."

The Wings started 7–7 in their new home. Soon afterward they went through an 11-game losing streak. They finished 11–23.

They did better in 2017, with a 16–18 record. Guard Allisha Gray was named WNBA Rookie of the Year. She averaged 13 points a game. By now the WNBA had a new playoff format. The top 8 of the league's 12 teams qualified. The first two rounds were each a single game. The Wings played the Mystics in the first round. They lost 86–76.

Two months into the 2018 season, the Wings stood 14–9. Then they had a nine-game losing streak. They finished 15–19. In her third stint with the team, center Liz Cambage set a new WNBA single-game scoring record with 53 points. The Wings met the Mercury in the first round. Phoenix broke open a tight game in the third

LIZ CAMBAGE
CENTER
HEIGHT: 6-FOOT-8
SHOCK/WINGS SEASONS:
2011, 2013, 2018

FINDING HER WAY

Growing up in Australia, Liz Cambage was bullied. She said, "I was made to feel like a freakish monster for being tall and a person of color." (Her father is Nigerian, and her mother is Australian.) At first Cambage wasn't interested in sports. Her mother urged her to play basketball. She made the Australian national junior women's team when she was 17. The Shock made her the second overall pick in the 2011 WNBA Draft. She was named to the WNBA All-Rookie First Team and the All-Star Game. But she was unhappy. Living in Tulsa was a culture shock. "I cried every day," she said. She skipped the 2012 season. Cambage came back in 2013. She improved her scoring and rebounding numbers. She was still unhappy. She left again and played overseas for several years. Wings coach Fred Williams persuaded her to return in 2018. She led the league in scoring.

DALLAS WINGS

Allisha Gray

quarter. The Mercury went on to an easy 101–83 victory. Dallas lost the first five games in 2019. They never came close to breaking even and finished 10–24.

The COVID-19 pandemic forced major changes in 2020. The season started late and consisted of 22 games, rather than the usual 34. Every game was played in Bradenton, Florida. No fans were allowed. The Wings finished 8–14. They missed the playoffs.

The 2021 season was back to normal with a full slate of games. After a 9–9 mark a month and a half into the season, the Wings faded and finished 14–18. That was still good enough for the playoffs. They faced Chicago. The eventual champion Sky defeated them 81–64.

The Wings flew out to a 5–2 start in 2022. They fell to 12–16 late in the season. At that point they won six of their final eight games to finish 18–18 and earn the 6-seed in the playoffs. Two-time All-Star guard Arike Ogunbowale was among the league leaders in scoring with an average of 19.7 points per game. Las Vegas coach Becky Hammon called center Teaira McCowan the "Monster in the Middle" in her first season with Dallas. She had a strong second half of the season to finish with an average of 11 points per game. Dallas lost Game 1 of the best-of-three first-round playoff series against the Connecticut Sun. The Wings came back to win Game 2, 89–79. It was their first playoff win since moving to Dallas in 2015. But the Sun won Game 3, 73–58.

The Dallas Wings have not enjoyed much success since leaving Detroit. They have been especially noted for long losing streaks. Fans hope that the team will rebound to its Detroit dynasty days and add another championship banner to the three they already hold.

Teaira McCowan

INDEX